COME UP DEEPER

Journeying Into the Secret Place of the Most High

Dr. Cislin Williams

Six Hearts
publishing

Come Up Deeper:

Journeying Into the Secret Place of the Most High

Text & Cover Design by Huntley Burgher
Published by Six Hearts Publishing
Davie, Florida 33328
www.sixheartspublishing.com

ISBN: 978-0-9845767-7-7
Library of Congress Control Number: 2011942472

Unless otherwise indicated,
scripture quotations used in this booklet
are from, The King James Version of the Bible (KJV).

Printed in the United States of America

Dedication

This book is dedicated to all those who desire to experience the presence of God.

Contents

Acknowledgements..7

Introduction..9

Chapter 1:   You Don't Have to Stay in the State You're In.........13

Chapter 2:   Trip vs. Journey...17

Chapter 3:   Moses... 31

Chapter 4:   Two Personal Stories...39

Chapter 5:   A Revelation of Worship..47

Chapter 6:   Bring a Willing Offering with the Heart.................53

Chapter 7:   Prepare a Consecrated Place for God's Presence

                to Reside...59

Chapter 8:   Secure your Travel Document................................65

Chapter 9:   You're Getting Closer...73

Chapter 10:   Get Ready to Experience a Third-Degree Burn......81

Chapter 11:   Go On In–It's Open...93

Notes...98

Acknowledgements

My heart-felt gratitude and thanks to my family and friends who stood by me throughout the years as I lived this experience. I am indeed grateful for your understanding and words of encourage-ment, but most of all for being patient with me.

I am forever indebted to my husband, Apostle Winston Williams whose belief in me has pushed me to the point of no return. Thanks for your love, support and guidance.

I could never have accomplished this milestone had it not been for my children's, Nicole and Winston Jr. encouraging words, "Mommy, you're the greatest." Thanks for believing in me.

Thanks Christopher. Your "I don't know what you're waiting for grandma" helped to make this possible. A great big 'thank you' to my granddaughter, Karris for bringing me drinks while I write.

I would be remiss, if I did not acknowledge my mother, Esther McAllister. Thanks mom for constantly cleaning up after me, while I work. I appreciate you more than words can tell.

Introduction

One would not try to go on a journey or take a trip before first deciding on the destination. You may not know how to get there just yet, but you know exactly where you want to go. With the advancement of technology, we now have several navigational systems that will direct us to our destination with specific guidance along the route.

The psalmist in Psalm 91 declares, "He that continues to dwell in the secret place of the Most High, shall abide under the shadow of the Almighty". A proper theological interpretation of this verse will reveal that it is making reference to Jesus, and through Him, we too can dwell in the secret place of the Most High. But the statement begs the question "Where is the secret place of the Most High? And how can I find it?" Throughout the pages of *"Come Up Deeper: Journeying into the Secret Place of the Most High"*, I seek to answer the question of, "where or what is the secret place of the Most High?" and to provide you with a spiritual GPS (God's Positioning System) to guide you on your journey.

We are embarking on a journey into His presence. This is a journey that will take us into the place where He dwells. Yes, I am well aware that His presence fills the universe. But there is a place in God where only those who seek will find it. There is a beautiful revelation of God's presence among men, recorded in a discourse between God and Moses.

Passage Exodus 33

11And the LORD spake unto Moses face to face, as a man speaketh unto his friend. …

12And Moses said unto the LORD, See, thou sayest unto me, Bring up this people: and thou hast not let me know whom thou wilt send with me. Yet thou hast said, I know thee by name, and thou hast also found grace in my sight.

13Now therefore, I pray thee, if I have found grace in thy sight, shew me now thy way, that I may know thee, that I may find grace in thy sight: and consider that this nation is thy people.

17And the LORD said unto Moses, I will do this thing also that thou hast spoken: for thou hast found grace in my sight, and I know thee by name.

18And he said, I beseech thee, shew me thy glory.

19And he said, I will make all my goodness pass before thee, and I will proclaim the name of the LORD before thee; and will be gracious to whom I will be gracious, and will shew mercy on whom I will shew mercy.

> ²⁰*And he said, Thou canst not see my face: for there shall no man see me, and live.*
>
> ²¹*And the LORD said, Behold, there is a place by me, and thou shalt stand upon a rock:*
>
> ²²*And it shall come to pass, while my glory passeth by, that I will put thee in a cleft of the rock, and will cover thee with my hand while I pass by:*
>
> ²³*And I will take away mine hand, and thou shalt see my back parts: but my face shall not be seen.*

On this journey God reveals His glory to us in the form of His presence among us. He allows us to find this place where we can have a deep abiding close intimate relationship with Him.

But why is this place a secret? It is a secret because it has been kept from the knowledge of any, except those who have been trained or afforded the honor. To be kept from the knowledge of some in no way indicates partiality or willful prevention on the part of God. It is more of a refusal on their part to be conversant with the truth that would supply that knowledge. It is hid from the eyes of those who refuse to see.

It is indeed an honor to enter into God's presence, but what training is involved? It is in the approach. There is a proper way to approach the secret place of the Most High. Throughout the book I will make references to the approach that was taught under the Old Covenant, and draw inferences from it as we search for parallels in the New Testament. My purpose is that we will apply the principles to our twenty-first century approach.

At the request of my family and close friends I have written *"Come Up Deeper: Journeying Into The Secret Place of the Most High"* so that hand in hand, we can take this journey together.

Come go with me. Let's take a journey into His presence.

Chapter 1
You Don't Have to Stay in the State You're In

When God first created man, He breathed into his nostril the breath of life and man became a living soul. By this action God awakened his consciousness and he became fully aware of his surroundings. He had a deposit of God within him and enjoyed communion with Him. Our Biblical records indicate that God would go down in the cool of the day to fellowship with man. Once Adam and his wife Eve sinned, they broke that communion with their Creator, and lost their paradise home.

After that garden tragedy, God had to keep them protected from His presence because in their fallen state they were unable to stand in the presence of a Holy God. Instead of God going down in the cool of the day to commune with them, they had to develop a thirst and a longing after God. It became necessary for man to 'seek' after God. The book of II Chronicles teaches that the path back to God begins with genuine repentance and a desire to restore God's original pattern. We gather from inferences made in the first five books of the Bible that God's original plan was to have fellowship with mankind.

In II Chronicles we have the account of Asa, one of Israel's kings, after he returned from waging war against the Ethiopians. The prophet of God approached him with a message. His exact words went out to Asa, and all Judah and Benjamin, " ...The Lord is with you, while you be with Him; and if you seek Him, He will be found of you; but if you forsake Him, He will forsake you." (15:2b). The prophet's message had a strong effect on Asa because he became bolder than he had ever been. Not only did he cleanse the land of idols but he caused the people to enter into a covenant to seek the Lord God with all their heart and with all their soul. The devastating consequence for anyone who would not seek the Lord God, was that they be put to death, whether they are man, or woman, small or great. The people did not shirk from hearing that announcement but entered into the covenant gladly, and with great rejoicing. They had made up minds. They swore to God with their whole hearts and sought Him with their whole desire. As a result of their solemn covenanting with God, He did well for them and gave them rest from their enemies round about.

God's answer for restoration in New Testament times is Jesus. On the night in which He was born wise men from the east followed a star to Bethlehem in search of the Christ child. We are well aware that He has long been removed from that manger in Bethlehem, but those of us who are wise, still seek Him. We long for Him and want to be in His presence daily. We desire more than a superficial acquaintance. We want to know Him and to enjoy a rich fellowship and communion with Him. As it were, we want to be wrapped up, tied up and tangled up in Him. So much so, that our every thought is directed by Him, and we live in full obedience to His words.

David, in Psalms 91, said that he that dwells in the secret place of the Most High shall abide under the shadow of the Almighty. The great truth that is revealed by this verse is that all those who live a life of communion with God are constantly safe under His protection. It is by faith that we find our repose in the secret place of the Most High. We acquaint ourselves with Him, through His word and time spent in His presence. It is the inner nature and character of a true believer to be at home in God. From the innermost recesses of our being we seek to worship Him and to be alone with Him. Not just superficially but a deep desire to be in His presence continually and to receive good from His hand.

The New Testament gospel accounts bear the record of a woman with an issue of blood for many years. She had such great faith despite the severity of her predicament that she pressed her way through a crowd that could have thronged her, to get close enough to the Master in order to touch the hem of His garment. She believed that if only she could accomplish this feat, she would be made whole and be rid of this malignity. She would once again be free to be in the physical presence of the Master unhindered. One songwriter says that in the presence of Jehovah troubles vanish. Why would we not then want to be in His presence continually?

There are so many issues that we encounter on a daily basis that it is rather unthinkable of anyone not wanting to be in His presence. Yet we find that being in the presence of God has become a far thought, even in the minds of professing believers. Some are even more eager to seek association with some high ranking dignitary than they are to seek a close relationship with the Almighty. We would all do well in seeking to dwell in the presence of the Most High God on a daily basis. Being close to Him and enjoying sweet fellowship and communion with Him should be our constant desire.

What troubling things are going on in your life right now?

Which of those things have been going on for a long time and with seemingly no answer in sight? Seek to be in His presence and watch those things vanish. There is absolutely no need to keep carrying a burden that you can be rid of. Take the trip from where you are right now, and get in His presence.

It's a journey worthwhile taking.

You don't have to stay in the state you're in.

Chapter 2
Trip Vs. Journey

There is a group of words in the English language that are used to indicate travel, each with its own shade of meaning and connotation. Nevertheless, they all indicate movement from one place to another. The place where you presently are, is not the place you desire to be, or to remain, therefore, you must progressively move in the direction of your desire. You are going to take a *trip,* or go on a *journey.*

There is not a vast difference in the meanings of these two words, and they are sometimes used interchangeably. The noun form of the word 'trip', according to several dictionaries is:

- A short journey
- An excursion

The word *trip* is a general word, indicating going any distance and returning, for either business or pleasure, and in either a hurried or a leisurely manner. It may or may not involve any planning and is usually done for a specific purpose. As is the case with, a quick trip to the store.

Journey signals a passage from one place to another and is sometimes applied figuratively to the passage through life. It usually indicates a trip of considerable length and is now applied to travel that is more leisurely or more fatiguing than a trip, furthermore a return is not necessarily indicated. Journey has adventure and involves planning. One of the key differences of the two words, however, is that whereas trip emphasizes the destination or the reason for travelling, *journey* focuses on the idea of travelling.

Often times as I child I would hear adults say "we need to stop and smell the roses". Needless to say I had no clue as to the meaning of the phrase. As I read many self-development books in my adult years, I have come across the phrase "Success is a journey, not a destination". I am beginning to understand from those two phrases that there are times in life in which we need to enjoy the process as well as the destination. Changing position from where you are now to enter into the secret place of the Most High, is a journey as well as a trip, in that -

- It does involve planning and preparation
- It can be a short distance, as well as a long distance
- The destination is important, and so is the travel itself
- You may return as well as, you may and should choose to dwell

IT DOES INVOLVE PLANNING AND PREPARATION

Taking a journey into the secret place of the Most High involves planning in the sense that, the individual so determined to do, have it in mind as a purpose. This is what I am going to do. The will or intention to carry out that action is present. Since this is a stated purpose and a desired goal, a strategy needs to be developed in order to realize its fulfillment. A vital part of any planning process is to have clearly defined objective(s). Without clearly defined objective(s), one will not be able to formulate a strategy, implement the strategy, evaluate the process and make necessary adjustments in order to stay on track. Another important aspect of the process leading to the fulfillment of a goal, is the time of preparation.

The book of Exodus describes the departure of the nation of Israel from their bondage in the land of Egypt. The story is told of how God led them on their journey by a pillow of cloud by day and fire by night. God's presence indicated by these two symbols was always with them. Leading them, guiding them and protecting them. On their long journey from Egypt to the Promised Land, Israel had now arrived at Mount Sinai, and God is about to reveal His plan to them through Moses their leader.

Exodus 19:10-11, 14-15

[10]And the LORD said unto Moses, Go unto the people, and sanctify them today and tomorrow, and let them wash their clothes,

[11]And be ready against the third day: for the third day the LORD will come down in the sight of all the people upon Mount Sinai

[14]And Moses went down from the mount unto the people, and sanctified the people; and they washed their clothes.

[15]And he said unto the people, Be ready against the third day: come not at your wives.

God's requirement prior to the plan being unfolded is that they should prepare themselves to receive it. The command to *sanctify* means to make oneself clean ceremonially as well as morally. They were to spend two days in purifying which included washing their clothes because on the third day they were going to have a visible appearance of God's glory. In essence God directed Moses to call the children of Israel off from their worldly business, and call them to religious exercises, meditation and prayer. Likewise us embarking on the ultimate trip of journeying into the secret place of the Most High, we need to sanctify ourselves and get ready beforehand. We need to gather up our wandering thoughts and bring them into subjection to the law of God in our hearts. We need to abandon all impure affections and quiet all inappropriate passions. All our cares about secular business must be laid aside as we prepare to approach our God.

They were told to wash their clothes. To them various washings were a part of ceremonial cleansing. For us today, it is a sign of dignity and respect for us to appear before great men in clean clothes. Since we are taking a trip into the secret place of the Most High, we should endeavor to appear before Him clean. Men see our clothes whether they are clean or not, but our most Heavenly Father sees our hearts. We should prepare to wait upon Him with clean hearts, cleansed by the words which Jesus spoke to us as recorded in the Bible.

In token of total surrender to the Most High God, and preparing to enjoy Him and Him only, they should also abstain from approaching their wives. To take a trip into the secret place of the Most High, the traveller has to have a mind made up to seek Him and Him alone. Enjoy Him and Him alone. Crave after Him and Him alone. Seek to be satisfied by Him and Him alone. No other satisfaction is necessary, or should be sought. This is a worthwhile preparation if one is to enjoy the full benefit of the journey.

IT CAN BE A SHORT DISTANCE, AS WELL AS
A LONG DISTANCE

Both of my children are now adults who live away from home. They both reside in the same city about an hour from each other. I am always amused to listen to my son complain that my daughter lives too far, and he has to condition his mind to take a road trip whenever he goes to see her. On one occasion while I was spending time in their city, I decided to stay with my daughter because she has my two grandchildren. My son was forced to come by to see me. As we were discussing over dinner, he again brought up the subject of my daughter's residence being far. So I asked him, "far from what?" His response was that the statement he has been making for a long while now, is a rather subjective one, so he wishes to clarify. He continued by saying that due to the fact that his field of endeavor requires much travel, he chooses to live close to the airport, so in reference to the airport, my daughter lives far.

If my intention is to be close to the airport in that city, then it would be rather nonsensical for me to stay with my daughter. When it's time for me to travel back home, the trip to the airport from my son's residence is considerably shorter than the trip from my daughter's home. With the airport as my point of reference then, the proximity to it would depend on where I had chosen to reside.

Throughout this discourse, I am pre-supposing that individuals are interested in taking the trip into the secret place of the Most High. The distance they travel will depend largely on where they have been residing. It can be as fast as a quick trip to the community corner store, as well as it may be the long journey to the city for suburban residents. Because, this is an adventure of going deeper and deeper into and through the soul to reach the spirit which communes with God, then the trip really depends on the condition of the mind of the seeker. If the mind has not been trained to seek after the things of God and to commune with Him daily, then that seeker has a longer distance, so to speak, than a mind that has been in fellowship and communication with Him on a consistent basis.

The story is told in Luke 18 of a Publican (a tax collector) and a Pharisee (a member of a segregated religious sect) who went up to the temple to pray. The Pharisee stood and prayed proudly to himself, while the Publican showed much humility in his prayer. The record is that the Publican was more justified than the Pharisee, and was better received. The Lord removes himself far from the proud but gives heed to the humble.

If one lives in a state of elevated pride and has a desire to take the journey into the secret place of the Most High, they will indeed have a long distance to travel. Because firstly, they would need to be rid of their pride in order to have a proper focus. It is important to remember that all we have and is and ever will be is all because of Christ. A haughty spirit precedes a fall and one cannot afford to keep tripping on this journey. Rid yourself of a puffed up spirit, then start the journey into the secret place of the Most High.

Many self-development teachers and motivational speakers teach that our attitude determines our altitude. In the case of the two seekers in the temple, the Pharisee did not get very close to God, because of his pride. On this journey to the secret place of the Most High, one who is proud has a farther distance to travel than one who humbles himself and approaches God with a heart of humility.

The Apostle Paul, writing to the Ephesians reiterated that they were in a miserable condition before they received the message of salvation. They were in fact afar off. But once they were taught, they were brought near through the blood of Jesus Christ. Like the Ephesians and all others who have received the teachings of Christ and given heed to them, if you have the desire to take the journey into the secret place of the Most High, you too can be brought near through the finished work of Jesus Christ. What was once a long journey for all of us, can be and is now a very short one. We each individually make the decision.

The prodigal son, in the gospel of St. Luke, was living with his father and enjoying the benefits of being a son. He made the decision to remove himself from his father's covering and wondered afar off. After much hardship, he one day made the decision to return home. Even though he had to take a long trip back home, he decided to embark on the journey. The record of this story reported that his father who was awaiting his return, saw him coming afar off and ran to meet him. Once you make the decision to get into the secret place of the Most High, God will supply you with the necessary grace to make the journey. He is awaiting your move towards Him and will run to meet you and escort you in.

If one intended to embark on a trip before the advent of GPS (Global Positioning Satellite) systems and Google maps, they would make a visit to their nearest AAA (American Automobile Association) location to pick up a map, or to the department store to purchase a 'Randy McNally' map. If their choice was AAA, the customer service representative would chart their course for them and highlight it with a brightly colored marker, informing them that if they followed the marking, they should have no problem making their trip successfully. Armed with map in hand and full confidence in the advice of the AAA representative, they would embark on their journey. As long as they stayed on course, they would make it to their destination. If they veered off course, or encountered a detour, they ran the risk of adding miles to their trip. The more off course detours that they voluntarily do, or are forced to do, the more miles they would add.

The path to the secret place is mapped out for us in the 'Basic Instructions Before Leaving Earth'. Follow it, and you are guaranteed a successful journey.

THE DESTINATION IS IMPORTANT, AND SO IS THE TRAVEL ITSELF

In the early 1990's, I remember going on a thirteen hundred mile road trip from Florida to Philadelphia. We packed up a SUV and started out in the early morning hours before sunrise. Our destination was of course, Philadelphia but we decided early on that we were going to make several stops along the way and enjoy the journey while we travelled. We could have made the trip in one day, stopping only for gas and food. However, we stopped for as long as we desired and took our time getting to our destination. Throughout our two-day travel we enjoyed some memorable moments.

We stopped to view and take pictures of the sunrise. Along the way, we stopped to enjoy a meal in a little country town hamburger shack. Those were some of the biggest hamburgers I had ever seen. We stopped for dinner that night in another place and were amazed by the size of the plates and the amount of food the servers were able to stack on top of them. We had to look around the food in order to get eye contact with each other while we dined. We were even more amazed at the cost. We were able to figure out that what we were accustomed to paying for dining out in Florida for one night, could have fed us for almost a week in this country town. Needless to say we pondered the thought of relocating, which we now joked of doing for a few hours overnight. We were bound and determined to enjoy every aspect of that trip. We decided to stop and smell the roses, if not all, a great many of them.

With seven of us travelling, we had four teenagers in the group, and a two-year old who just wanted to know "are we there yet?" every ten minutes, or so it seemed. Each teen wanted to listen to their choice of music. We had our own choices as adults and truly abhorred their music. Technology being what it was back then, we did not have the luxury of iPods and iPads, so we had to make a compromise from time to time on the radio station that we tuned in to, or whose cassette tape we played. Nevertheless, with all of this going on we had a truly memorable trip. The teachable moments and the moments of excitement far outweighed the minor glitches we had. We enjoyed the trip.

As we drove up to grandma's house and smelled the scent of grandma's cooking and saw her at the gate welcoming us with out-stretched arms, we knew we had reached our destination. Just to be at grandma's house, we knew we were in for a great big treat and we were going to enjoy being there immensely. But our memory of this trip was not just what we did at grandma's house, but everything we experienced from the moment we prayed our initial prayer for a safe trip, until we prayed a prayer of thanksgiving for bringing us there safely.

Once you make the decision to take the journey into the secret place of the Most High, get ready to enjoy the trip as well as the destination. At first this journey consists of baby steps because you are growing and developing in grace. As you take each step, enjoy the moment and celebrate the victory. You are being changed into

Christlikeness, so you are surrendering your ways of doing things and learning His ways. You also have to make the decision as to what to take with you on this journey. Like a runner in a race, you are going to find that this journey requires you to strip down to the bare essentials. With each thing that you lay aside, you are going to marvel at the experience and the reward you receive in return. You are going to marvel at how you could have, and why did you travel with this impediment for so long.

When you begin to surrender your selfish motives and sinful desires, you will experience such joy and a peace that surpasses all human understanding.

Celebrate each moment.

YOU MAY RETURN AS WELL AS YOU MAY AND SHOULD CHOOSE TO DWELL

When we took that trip to grandma's house, we stayed for a few days and returned home. We wanted to stay with grandma and she also hated to see us leave. However sad the parting was, we parted. Living on this earth, and having to deal with the cares of life and our various responsibilities, taking up residence at grandma's house was not feasible. We could have chosen to ignore our responsibilities and disregard wisdom and stay with grandma, but that would have been poor judgment on our part. So instead of dwelling with grandma, we choose to return home. Even before we left grandma's driveway, we stared to miss grandma's presence, her cooking, her stories and just her love and warmth, and she missed our company as well. But that was the choice we made.

Should you decide to take the journey into the secret place

of the Most High, you should also make the decision to surrender your all to the Master and to dedicate your life to Him in devoted service. He takes no pleasure in those who draw nigh unto Him in lip service only but their hearts are far from Him. In the same way in which he would go down in the cool of the day to commune with Adam and Eve, He desires you to stay in constant communication with Him. None of us know how to chart our own course, because we do not know the way into the secret place of the Most High. Jesus came to show us the way back to the Father and to be the door by which we enter. The Father provided us with the Holy Spirit to be our guide throughout the journey.

It is futile to get to a place of spiritual maturity and enjoy the benefits of such; love, peace, joy, contentment and a whole host of other spiritual benefits, and to leave that place to return to a life devoid of the richness of His grace. As foolish as it is, it remains your choice to make. Are you going to leave this place of spiritual bliss once you get there to return to moral degradation? or, are you planning on making this a way of life? You may return, as well as you may choose to dwell. Which is it going to be?

Unlike the trip to grandma's house, you do not have to return to the place you called home. God will take care of everything that concerns you should you choose to dwell with Him.

Allow me to exercise my literary privileges here as I personalize psalm 91:

Seeing that I have made the choice to dwell in the secret place of the Most High;

- *I am guaranteed His protection.*

- *He has become my refuge and my fortress*

because I placed my trust in Him.

- *He has delivered me from the snare of the fowler and from the noisome pestilence.*

- *He has protected me like a hen protects her chickens.*

- *His truth has become my shield and buckler.*

- *I am not afraid of the terror that chooses to attack at night, neither am I afraid of all the arrows that are hurled at me throughout the day.*

- *No pestilence or destruction whether in darkness or in light shall make me afraid.*

- *I know that even though others are getting hurt by the thousands and ten thousand, none of those destructions shall come near to me.*

- *I will behold the destruction of the wicked with my eyes.*

- *I am safe from evil and plagues, because He has assigned and instructed angels to guard me at all times.*

- *I have guidance for all my ways.*

- *I have dominion over every fierce beast or*

> *animal. It is my right and authority to trample them under my foot.*

- *I have set my love upon the Most High, and when I call, He will answer me.*

- *If I ever get in trouble, I know of a surety that He will deliver me.*

- *He will satisfy me with long life, so nothing or no one can cut my life short.*

You may choose to make this your personal affirmation.

With this guarantee, why wouldn't I want to dwell with Him? Why wouldn't you? Why wouldn't anyone?

Chapter 3
Moses

God in His sovereignty choose to reveal much of Himself to mankind through His relationship with the children of Israel. The second half of the book of Exodus, outlines the regulations that would govern the lives of the children of Israel under what is now known as the Old Covenant. All of the laws and practices in that Old Covenant were a shadow of things to come. They served as a school master pointing the way to a better covenant which was delivered in Jesus Christ.

A proper study of theology will reveal that as twenty first century Christians, we should not disregard the Old Testament scriptures on the premise that Jesus came so they are done away with. Jesus came and brought a New Covenant, a better deal, but not to destroy the old. He fulfilled the Old Testament scriptures not destroy them. He fulfilled them in that He satisfied them fully by performing perfect obedience to them. Something that man was incapable of doing. To destroy them would be to render them useless and ineffective which He never did. There is much to be learned from the Old Testament scriptures.

The number one thing that God wanted to do and still wants

to do with His children is to establish a close, intimate personal relationship with them. We want to look for a while at the great leader Moses whom God choose to lead the children of Israel from Egypt's bondage to their dwelling in the Promised Land.

Exodus 33:11a

¹¹And the LORD spake unto Moses face to face, as a man speaketh unto his friend...

Deuteronomy 34:10

¹⁰And there arose not a prophet since in Israel like unto Moses, whom the LORD knew face to face,

Moses is famous for his intimate acquaintance with God, as revealed by the record of him in the foregoing scriptures, so we want to particularly take a closer look at his journey into the secret place of the Most High.

At the time of his birth a cruel law was set in place by the Egyptian leaders commanding the murder of all Hebrew male children. His mother gave birth to him and observed him to be a goodly child. His beauty far surpassed the ordinary and his parents regarded this as some kind of an indication of a purpose from God. His parents were determined not to have him destroyed, and managed to keep him hidden for a while until it was no longer safe to do so. His mother decided to let fate have its course, by preparing a basket in which to set him afloat on the river Nile. God knowing the plans he had for him, caused him to be rescued by Pharaoh's daughter. She provided a home for him in the palace and raised him as her son, with his mother being his nurse.

Moses had now passed the first forty years of his life in Pharaoh's courts being prepared for business. One day he wandered out into the fields and observed injustice being done to a Hebrew at the hands of an Egyptian. After he surveyed his surroundings, and concluded that no one else was present, he reacted to the incident by murdering the Egyptian and hiding his body in the sand. The following day he went out and saw two Hebrews smiting each other. To his astonishment when he drew near to help, one of them ridiculed him for the murder he committed the previous day. The news of this happening reached the ears of Pharaoh and he sought to slay Moses, but he escaped from Pharaoh and travelled to the land of Midian. He met and married one of the daughters of a Midianite priest and began working as a shepherd.

Here is a man, that unknown to him at this point had started out on a journey to be drawn into the secret place of the Most High. He was about to enter another phase of his preparation and planning for the long trip.

Exodus 3: 1-6

¹Now Moses kept the flock of Jethro his father in law, the priest of Midian: and he led the flock to the backside of the desert, and came to the mountain of God, even to Horeb.

²And the angel of the LORD appeared unto him in a flame of fire out of the midst of a bush: and he looked, and, behold, the bush burned with fire, and the bush was not consumed.

³And Moses said, I will now turn aside, and see this great sight, why the bush is not burnt.

⁴And when the LORD saw that he turned aside to see, God called unto him out of the midst of the bush, and said, Moses, Moses. And he said, Here am I.

⁵And he said, Draw not nigh hither: put off thy shoes from off thy feet, for the place whereon thou standest is holy ground.

⁶Moreover he said, I am the God of thy father, the God of Abraham, the God of Isaac, and the God of Jacob. And Moses hid his face; for he was afraid to look upon God.

His first encounter with God, aroused his curiosity, but startled him nonetheless.

In Egypt, Moses learned to be a scholar, a gentleman, a statesman and a soldier. This prepared him to rule in places of government. However, he lacked the training and experience of what it means to live a life of communion with God. In order for Moses to fulfill the assignment God planned for him, as the leader of this mass multitude of Israelites, he had to keep in close communication with God. God in his providential wisdom gave him a 'crashcourse', by allowing him to tend sheep. This job taught him solitude and prepared him to converse with God in mount Horeb. He learned how to be alone with God, a lesson that would serve him well in his future assignment. God gave him the assignment and the power to lead His chosen people out of Pharaoh's bondage. He received specific instructions and preparation for the task at hand. To Moses, the journey into the secret place of the Most High started with him rendering service to his fellowmen.

When communication is started with us and God, it will never fail on His part. Moses had now grown accustomed to approaching God to receive instructions at His hand. God called Moses in His presence once again, but this time he is to bring his working team with him, who will worship afar off but Moses alone will draw near.

Exodus 24

> *¹And he said unto Moses, Come up unto the LORD, thou, and Aaron, Nadab, and Abihu, and seventy of the elders of Israel; and worship ye afar off.*

> *²And Moses alone shall come near the LORD: but they shall not come nigh; neither shall the people go up with him.*

> *⁹Then went up Moses, and Aaron, Nadab, and Abihu, and seventy of the elders of Israel:*

> *¹⁰And they saw the God of Israel: and there was under his feet as it were a paved work of a sapphire stone, and as it were the body of heaven in his clearness.*

> *¹¹And upon the nobles of the children of Israel he laid not his hand: also they saw God, and did eat and drink.*

Those who seek to journey into the secret place of the Most High, must ever be mindful of the fact that God has condescended in order for us to draw near. We must enter worshipfully and be guided by His direction. Moses and his company did as was required and they all saw the God of Israel.

Moses was further commissioned –

Exodus 24

> [12]And the LORD said unto Moses, Come up to me
> into the mount, and be there: and I will give thee
> tables of stone, and a law, and commandments
> which I have written; that thou mayest teach
> them.

> [13]And Moses rose up, and his minister Joshua:
> and Moses went up into the mount of God.

> [14]And he said unto the elders, Tarry ye here for
> us, until we come again unto you: and, behold,
> Aaron and Hur are with you: if any man have
> any matters to do, let him come unto them.

> [15]And Moses went up into the mount, and a cloud
> covered the mount.

> [16]And the glory of the LORD abode upon mount
> Sinai, and the cloud covered it six days: and the
> seventh day he called unto Moses out of the midst
> of the cloud.

> [17]And the sight of the glory of the LORD was like
> devouring fire on the top of the mount in the eyes
> of the children of Israel.

> [18]And Moses went into the midst of the cloud, and

> *gat him up into the mount: and Moses was in the*
> *mount forty days and forty nights.*

He was told to come up into the mountain and be there. No time schedule was given, just be there. Expect to stay for some time. Those who have decided to take the journey into the secret place of the Most High, must expect to spend some time in communion with Him. Just be there, even if He is not speaking, quiet your soul on the journey. The desires of your soul if not fully submitted to God will entice you to break communion with Him to tend to the needs of your lesser appetites. On this journey, spirit, soul and body must be totally committed. There must be absolutely no distractions. Moses sat waiting each day, not knowing which day God would speak to him further.

You cannot grow impatient or weary in waiting on the Lord. If Moses had grown tired before the seventh day and quit, he would not have been in position to receive the honor of being called further into the presence of the Most High. Communion with God is worth waiting for and it is only fitting that you should take time to compose yourselves for the entry. On the seventh day God called Moses up into the cloud and kept him there for forty days and forty nights. We can only imagine the revelation of the glory of God that Moses received. The people said that his face glowed when he re-entered the camp. During this time of being enveloped by the presence of the Most High, Moses received instructions for the pattern of a Tabernacle that was to be constructed in the wilderness. God also revealed to him His intention for this Tabernacle.

It is worthy of note that although God initiated contact with Moses, he was not scared to enter into His presence, unlike the children of Israel who asked him to speak to God on their behalf. It was his curiosity on the back side of the desert that led him to draw near to the burning bush. He was willing to turn aside from the task he was engaged in to see this great sight. When the Lord saw that he turned aside to see, God called out to him from the burning bush, and commanded him to take his shoes from off his feet. He gladly obeyed the command and later accepted the invitation to serve. From that time on he grew to know his God and enjoyed his presence. Moses had a life that was totally surrendered to God. He was not afraid to enter into a close intimate relationship with God.

The manifested presence of God can be a startling reality as well as a beautiful experience. Once you have made the decision to follow the path into the secret place of the Most High, be prepared to experience the glory of God. There is nothing on earth to compare. I have had the blessing of experiencing the incredible manifestation of His presence, and I can personally attest to the fact that this kind of supernatural activity at first can be scary. I hasten to empathize with the children of Israel who were startled by the appearance of His glory. After having had this experience several times, I assure you there is absolutely no reason to be afraid.

Take this journey into the secret place of the Most High in faith. Expect God to meet you along the way and guide you the rest of the way. It's an experience second to none on this side of heaven.

Chapter 4
Two Personal Stories

For well over two decades now, I have taken time out alone for fasting, prayer and meditation. These are times when I seclude myself from all outside interferences and remain quiet to meditate and reflect on my life and ministry and to receive instructions for the journey forward. Those times have brought tremendous clarity to some things that I may have misunderstood or overlooked, together with divine revelations and insight into the word of God. I look forward to taking these trips and the more I do them is the more I want to do them. In fact I have gotten to the place where I just want to stay in that place. It has now become a lifestyle.

For each trip I am given specific instructions prior to going. The instructions vary from time to time, but the one constant instruction for every trip is that I remain in the place where I have chosen to retreat and not to go in and out. I am always forbidden to leave until the time of my seclusion is ended. On these trips, if at no other time in my spiritual walk, I am totally submitted to the leading of the Holy Spirit. God is totally in control. I have no desire for anything but God. I want to take a moment here to recall an incident that at first I considered valueless, simply because it was contrary to instructions that I'd been given on all previous trips.

RITZ CRACKERS

Less than an hour after being dropped off at a local hotel to begin one of these solitary retreats, I had an insatiable desire for some Ritz crackers. The desire was so pressing that I could not concentrate on anything but to satisfy it. It was as if an invisible force was driving, no, rather pushing me. I decided to make a quick trip to the hotel gift shop. Because I felt as if I was disobeying a command, I prayed that the Holy Spirit would not count the time when I was gone as a part of the retreat, but that the period of this retreat would start after I return. I quickly made my way to the hotel gift shop.

To my utter amazement and horror, the gift shop had no Ritz crackers. The store attendant suggested that I go seek some from the dining room staff who were preparing for lunch. When I got to the dining room, the attendant and I had a language barrier, because even though years ago I had studied French, I was unable to communicate it fluently at a most needed time. I wish I knew how to ask for Ritz crackers in French. To no avail I tried to indicate to the attendant what I wanted. Growing more and more ashamed of my action, and also the disappointment and frustration I was then feeling, I returned to the gift shop. After painting a rather distressing picture for the attendant, she was very eager and anxious to help. After all, who wouldn't sympathize with a damsel in distress? As if she suddenly remembered, she informed me that there was a supermarket just outside the hotel.

Needless to say, I was now at the point of no return. I was being pushed beyond limit. It was then one o'clock in the afternoon in over ninety degree heat that I made the decision to go fetch some Ritz crackers quickly and get back to my room. This did not seem like a big task at the moment, because after all, the supermarket was "just outside the hotel", in the exact words of the gift shop attendant. My assumption was that the supermarket was immediately behind the hotel, as I did not recall seeing one on my way driving in. To my amazement, when I got to the end of the walkway, there was no supermarket in sight. I got out on the roadway and as far as my eyes could see, there was no building that remotely resembled a supermarket.

By this time, the driving force behind this desire caused me to reason that since I was already outside, I should find the super- market regardless of wherever it was. It appeared as a tiny speck on the horizon. Like a deer panting after water, I set my sights on reaching it. After a thirty-minute walk in the scorching sun, with improper attire, I finally reached my destination. All that was left to finalize my goal now, was to have the object of my desire in hand. Still trying to do this as fast as I could, I made my way hur- riedly through the aisles in this unfamiliar territory. I finally spot- ted crackers. I grabbed a box from the shelf, paid the cashier and dashed out of the supermarket for the thirty minute walk back, which I intended to do in less time.

Because I felt that I was in a disobedient mode, I further de- cided that since I've already messed up, I should complete the act by having some of my most recent acquisition with a cup of tea and officially start the retreat at the end of the meal. I picked up the box, and was slapped as it were with an overwhelming disappoint- ment – I had the wrong crackers. And to top it all off, it was a diet version of whatever crackers it was. It tasted horrible. I was not about to leave the room again so I placed the stack of crackers back in the box with a sinking feeling in my stomach. I had disobeyed a direct command, and for what purpose?

Just as I was about to sit down and brood, I sensed the urge to pick up my pen and paper. I certainly was not about to journal this act, because I really did not want to have any long term memory of this behavior. The inner voice of the Holy Spirit had me to pen these words:

> "When God calls you into His presence it is a time to worship. He should be the object of your desire and nothing else. In the same way that you had an insatiable desire to satisfy your lesser appetite, and nothing could deter you from doing so, you should have even a greater desire to satisfy your spiritual appetite. The desire for food to satisfy a lesser appetite should not over power the desire to satisfy a greater appetite – that of being in the presence of the Almighty."

What I considered to be my disobedience to a direct command, God used as an object lesson. He gave me a revelation of what it means to worship which I will share with you in the chapters to follow.

The spirit within you longs for God, and desires Him. Your spirit wants to pull you into the secret place of the Most High. Fight against anything that seeks to pull you away and cling to that which pulls you in - worship.

FRAGRANCE OF CHRIST

I have been asked on many occasions if I would allow others to accompany me on these trips. Because I cherish these times and hold them dear to my heart, I felt as if it would have been an intrusion to grant any such request. The folks that surround me said that I return with a glow from these trips, and usually when given an occasion to speak after such trips, the wealth of the revelation and visible anointing was staggering. They kept insisting that since I do not want to take them with me, I should teach them how to do it on their own. I have found, and strongly believe, that the best way to teach is to model behavior and to allow the participants to be actively involved in their own learning.

It was on the foregoing belief that on one occasion I gathered together a group of women for an eighteen-hour 'shut-in'. I figured that I would let them have a taste of what it takes to be still before the Lord, with no personal agenda. In the event that they were unable to do an eighteen hour shut in with other women, then I would know for sure, they would not be able to withstand seven days alone. We started the shut in at 10:00pm that night with the intention of discussing *The Tabernacle in the Wilderness,* coupled with praise and worship as well as corporate and individual prayer throughout the night. And believe it or not, a three-hour quiet time, or rest period. There was no restriction on what those three hours were used for. We reassembled at 6:00am for prayer and praise. After that time, there was a break for the women to refresh themselves for the day. As the leader and facilitator of the group, I decided that I would allow all the women to refresh themselves and return to the meeting room, after which I would be the last to refresh. I instructed them to be in silent meditation and worship while I was away. I remember specifically asking them to avoid the use of make-up and strong perfumes at this time. In retrospect, I believe that was a divine set-up.

As I reentered the room, I smelled the strong scent of perfume, a very sweet fragrance. I concluded that someone had disobeyed my instructions and now the room was filled with whatever they've been using. As I proceeded to interrogate them, they all denied that they had done what I was accusing them of and offered for me to smell the lotions that some of them had used to moisturize their hands. Like the leader of a communist party I actually took them up on the offer to smell the lotions, trying to identify the 'culprit' as it were. After about the fourth lotion, I apologized to them because I could not identify the smell in any of the lotions. The fragrance filled the air and everyone in the room was experiencing the scent so they were able to attest to the fact that none of their lotions had a similar smell.

I approached a vase to detect if the scent was coming from the flowers, when the Holy Spirit gently ridiculed me. He reminded me, that years ago prior to this event, I was praying with a missionary to India, when the room was suddenly filled with a sweet fragrance. It was at that point that I was embarrassed, firstly because as I had already sunken my face into the flowers and it was then that I remembered that they were artificial. Secondly, the Savior we had gathered to meet, showed up and we, I in particular, did not recognize His presence. We have worshipped and prayed all night asking Him to reveal Himself to us, yet when He did, we were startled.

Without any more being said everyone remained silent. On one accord, as if we were a choir or an orchestra being led by a conductor, we all bowed our faces to the ground. The scent continued among us for over three hours. There were spontaneous utterances of praise and worship. Some of us were crying, some singing songs in languages they had never learned, some laughing, some uttering groans, some just remained silent. All were worshipping in their own unique expressions of adoration.

The remainder of what transpired throughout that time, I will definitely have to say like Daniel and the three Hebrew boys to the king, "I am not careful to answer you in this matter." I now understand Peter, James and John's inability to relate in details what happened on the Mount of Transfiguration. It is virtually impossible to describe a heavenly experience satisfactorily in earth's languages. One has to have his very own experience.

I hasten now to share with you the revelation I received on that day in the summer of 2004. It will reveal to you the proper approach into the secret place of the Most High and cause you to experience His presence.

Chapter 5
A Revelation of Worship

To worship God, is to love Him and pursue Him devotedly. It is your willing response to the love of God, and it cannot be commanded. It is a time where your spirit touches God. He is a spirit and they that worship Him must do so in spirit and in truth (John 4:24). Flesh cannot worship God because it is earth bound and easily distracted. Rather than propelling you heavenward, it keeps you restricted to the things of the world. Your spirit, which is that immaterial, invisible part of you, will always be reaching to connect with the immaterial invisible God. The breath in you knows its source, and knows also that there is more remaining at the source.

At creation God breathed just a small fraction of Himself into man's nostrils. The best is yet to come. We have an earnest of our expectation, a deposit only. Our natural man has to be elevated to this place of worship. Like a dog on a leach pulling its master on a walk, so is your spirit pulling your mind and body to that elevated place of worship. Your spirit seeks nothing but to be in the presence of God. Your body and mind must become subject to the leading of the spirit to get you to the place of true worship. You will be drawn into the secret place of the Most High. In that worship experience you will lose all desire for anything but God. You long for God and Him alone, nothing else matters. There will be no desire to satisfy any of your lesser cravings.

In the same manner that the body will cause you to go in search of food to satisfy a natural craving, so will your spirit propel you towards the Lord and nothing will hinder you until your spirit is satisfied. There will be an intense desire to commune with the Lord. The Bible says that wherever your treasure is, there will your heart be also (Mt 6:21). Your heart is the center of your innermost being, and the word is used interchangeably with your spirit. Therefore, your spirit will always be pulling towards God, and seeking to worship. Your spirit wants to reside in His presence, because nowhere else will feel like home.

I have written this book on the premise that you do have an intense desire to experience God in His fullness. Not just to be on the surface hitting the top of the waves but to get into His abiding presence and remain in constant fellowship with Him. Like Peter, James and John, you want to be in His presence continually, so that you will miss nothing. You want to rest in His closeness at all times. Those three disciples got so close to Jesus on the Mount of Transfiguration, and saw things that none of the other disciples saw, that they were forever changed as a result. They have seen Jesus in all His glory. They were so awe struck that they were at a loss for the right words to say, neither could they relate what they had seen once they got down from the mountain. Jesus took them on a journey into the secret place of the Most High, and they were forever changed. John was transformed from an aggressive self-centered individual to be called the pillar of the Jerusalem church and the "apostle of love." From a desire to rain fire down on a village in Samaria that refused to accept Jesus, James later understood the purpose for Jesus' mission and submitted to it. Peter's enthusiasm which led him to go too far at times, was transformed into allowing him to be a spokesman for the Christian movement and the apostle to preach the first evangelistic sermons.

The Apostle Paul had similar experiences. He relates them far better that I can, so allow him to tell you one of his stories.

2 Corinthians 12

> *¹It is not expedient for me doubtless to glory. I will come to visions and revelations of the Lord.*
>
> *²I knew a man in Christ above fourteen years ago, (whether in the body, I cannot tell; or whether out of the body, I cannot tell: God knoweth;) such an one caught up to the third heaven.*
>
> *³And I knew such a man, (whether in the body, or out of the body, I cannot tell: God knoweth;)*
>
> *⁴How that he was caught up into paradise, and heard unspeakable words, which it is not lawful for a man to utter.*
>
> *⁵Of such an one will I glory: yet of myself I will not glory, but in mine infirmities.*
>
> *⁶For though I would desire to glory, I shall not be a fool; for I will say the truth: but now I forbear, lest any man should think of me above that which he seeth me to be, or that he heareth of me.*

One songwriter of old said, "There is a place of quiet rest near to the heart of God". I've found that place to be …

A place of victory over sin.

A place of joy.

A place of peace.

A place of excitement.

A place of fulfillment.

A place where purpose is revealed.

A resourceful place.

A hiding place.

A place of comfort and warmth.

A place of refreshing...

Oh the glory of His presence!

If you seek for such, let us take this *Journey Into The Secret Place of the Most High*. This is a trip that every child of God should be on continually. Never should we have a desire to be anywhere else. We should constantly be seeking to draw closer to Him and to reap the benefits of such closeness. It should be a way of life for all those who love Him.

Worship is an act of love and devotion to God. It is done by faith. It cannot be done in the flesh, because our flesh responds to its environment; the things that we see, smell, taste, hear and touch. Faith is not based on sight neither any of our other senses.

It is strictly on our belief and inner knowing. God whom we worship is invisible, and by faith we reach out to Him.

The way we live our lives will reveal the object of our love and devotion. If we are true worshippers of the Almighty God, we will seek to adhere to his revelatory truths and commands. Worship is not just a song we sing to the Lord. It is our reverence and adoration given to Him at all times. We don't 'come' to worship, we 'live' to worship. One twenty-first century songwriter sings:

> *To worship you I live (rep)*
> *I live to worship you.*

The very essence of our 'be-ing' is to worship the Father. We exist for that purpose and because of that everything we do should express our worship (adoration and love) for Him.

God will not leave us ignorant. He will and has taught us His ways. The principles of worship that will be shared in the remainder of this book are drawn from the form and principles of Israelite worship found throughout the book of Exodus. As modern-day readers of the Bible, we have a tendency to skim over or altogether avoid reading the detailed and often tedious texts of the Old Testament and focus instead on the simpler sections of the New Testament. With such a practice we would miss getting a comprehensive knowledge and understanding of Biblical theology.

If we are to enter into the secret place of the Most High, we must do it according to His prescription. So let us set our GPS (God's Positioning System) and get ready to embark on this journey into the presence of the Most High.

Chapter 6
Bring a Willing Offering With the Heart

Exodus 24

15And Moses went up into the mount, and a cloud covered the mount.

16And the glory of the LORD abode upon mount Sinai, and the cloud covered it six days: and the seventh day he called unto Moses out of the midst of the cloud.

17And the sight of the glory of the LORD was like devouring fire on the top of the mount in the eyes of the children of Israel.

18And Moses went into the midst of the cloud, and gat him up into the mount: and Moses was in the mount forty days and forty nights.

Exodus 25

¹And the LORD spake unto Moses, saying,

²Speak unto the children of Israel, that they bring me an offering: of every man that giveth it willingly with his heart ye shall take my offering.

⁸And let them make me a sanctuary; that I may dwell among them.

Your very offering is an act of worship, and how you do it reveals how much you honor God and desire His presence.

- It must be done willingly
- It must be offered from the heart
- The worshipper must 'bring' the offering unto the Lord.

Here Moses was instructed to speak unto the children of Israel to bring an offering that would be used to build a sanctuary for the Lord to dwell in. However, the instructions specifically said that Moses should receive it from those who brought it willingly with their heart.

The word used here to indicate 'willingness' is a Hebrew word that means:

- To incite
- To impel
- To do freely
- To give freely

The word has the flavor of an uncompelled, free movement of the will for divine service or sacrifice. It occurs seventeen times in the Old Testament and was especially used of volunteer soldiers.

The word used for 'heart' is more commonly interpreted as the totality of man's inner or immaterial nature. This usage has passed into common English with expressions such as:

- Heart and soul
- The heart goes out to someone
- His heart is in the right place
- From the bottom of our heart

In the Bible the whole spectrum of human emotions is attributed to the heart. It is almost a synonym for "mind". The heart is the seat of the will, so to refuse to make the proper decision is to harden the heart. Recall again Mt 6:21 "Where your treasure is, there will your heart be also". You will keep your mind on those things that you treasure.

The instruction was to bring the offering with the heart. Let the heart accompany the offering. This expression is referring to the inner state of those who contribute to the construction of the sanctuary. For us to experience the presence of the Lord, we have to build Him a place to dwell. We have to bring the material to be used with a willing heart.

You may have the experience of going into your neighborhoods to evangelize, and encounter those who want to give you an offering to take to the church. That is not done out of true worship to the Lord, but mostly as a means of getting rid of you and to have you going on your way. This person is not even attempting to embark upon the journey into the secret place of the Most High. For one, this individual has totally disconnected himself from his offering. His heart is not in it. If it were, he would be bringing it so that it accompanied his heart.

Let me hasten here to say that there are those who are physically handicapped or challenged and cannot literally 'bring' their offerings to an assembly of worshippers. Recall also that worship is a thing of faith, and an offering can be brought willingly from the heart even though the limbs cannot physically move. Also in this age of electronic transmittal, if taken literally, that too would pose a problem. The lesson here is that one does not separate himself from his offering unto a God he truly honors.

This idea of giving from the heart is also found in the New Testament Scriptures.

2 Corinthians 9

> *7Every man according as he purposeth in his heart, so let him give; not grudgingly, or of necessity: for God loveth a cheerful giver.*

The above-referenced scripture is part of the Apostle Paul's teachings to the Corinthians on giving. This in itself is a whole other book. However, we see here that it has to be an intention of the heart to give and not to do it grudgingly, which means *displaying or reflecting reluctance or unwillingness.*

In today's worship experience we are called upon to bring an offering in the same way that the Israelites were instructed to do so. We have gotten so far removed from God's original pattern so that we now "throw a collection" as it is referred to in some circles. And we do so without any regard or honor given unto the one to whom we pay homage. You desire to go up into His presence, and you do have to lay aside everything that so easily beset you on this journey. Human beings have a tendency to cling to things that should be so easy to give up. Rather than propelling us forward, they keep us stagnant, and most times pull us backwards. The one thing that I've noticed over the years that individuals are so willing to leave behind on this journey is an offering. And that is the one thing that ought not to be left behind. It is a display of poor manners to enter the presence of an earthly dignitary without bringing a gift. Some even bring a gift for the host of a house party or thanksgiving dinner. The Almighty God is far more honorable and dignified than any earthly creature.

On this journey into the secret place of the Most High to experience His presence, there is nothing that God should require of you that you refuse to give willingly. Please do not leave your 'pocket-book' on this journey. Bring it with you. Offering yourself to God, includes offering your substance and this is your very first act of worship, and it surely precedes your experiencing His presence.

Chapter 7

Prepare a Consecrated Place for God's Presence to Reside

As we take this journey into the secret place of the Most High, we will continue to look at some Old Testament references. We will seek to extract their true meanings and draw upon their parallels as they relate to us in the twenty-first century. We are seeking for applications, and not merely knowledge.

While Moses was up in the clouds for forty nights and forty days God gave him detailed instructions on how to build and furnish a sanctuary wherein He seeks to dwell. In this sanctuary God would manifest His presence among his children. Prior to this, there has never been a house designed and erected for that purpose. God knew that the children of Israel needed a visual representation of his presence among them. They demonstrated that fact when they made and worshipped a golden calf when Moses was up on the mountain for that extended period with the Lord.

Tabernacle means tent. This was a moveable tent made according to the pattern God gave Moses. The Israelites traveled with the Tabernacle and erected it in the wilderness whenever they pitched camp. The Tabernacle was more than just a dwelling place, it was an intricate design to illustrate God's relationship with man. The size, the color, the design, the furnishings; everything revealed some aspect of what God wanted us to know about Him and His plan for us. It was intended for a sign or a token of God's presence among His children. It was to be filled with the 'glory of the Lord' and by His presence there He would personally lead the children of Israel on their journey.   God revealed His visible presence among them by a pillar of cloud by day and a pillar of fire by night.

DIAGRAM OF THE FLOORPLAN OF THE TABERNACLE
(Not drawn to scale)

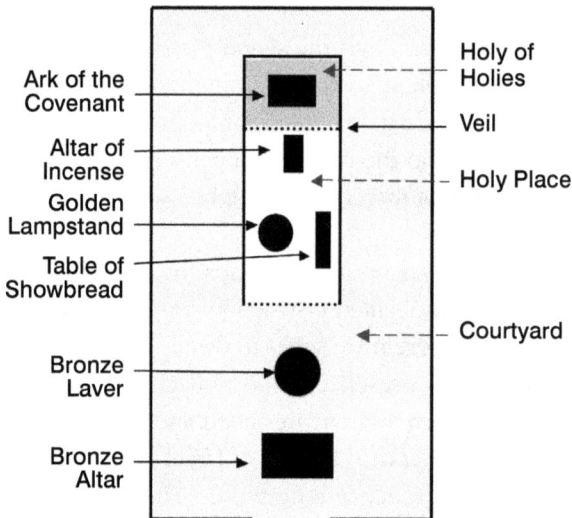

A thorough understanding of the significance of this Tabernacle has many practical benefits. However, to spend time elaborating on the intricate design of all the compartments and furnishings of this Tabernacle would cause us to take an unnecessary detour from the main subject of this book.   Nevertheless, we will strike the top of the waves in order to get enough understanding that will support the topic of our discussion. We will use it as a guide and an illustration as we continue on our journey into the secret place of the Most High. We will refer to various sections of this Tabernacle as we continue on our journey. For the remainder of this chapter, we will take a general look at the Tabernacle.

It was to be placed in the middle of the camp, signifying that it should be the center of all their activities. It was to be the place –

- Where they came to worship
- Where they consulted the oracles of God
- Where they would bring their sacrifices

The twelve tribes of Israel camped on the outside of the wilderness Tabernacle. Three tribes camped on the north, three on the south, three on the west and three on the east. We too are encompassed about, but we should remain centrally focused on the things of the spirit. We are sojourners in this world and we cannot escape the presence of others around us who do not share our beliefs. As we seek to enter into the secret place of the most High, we will be demonstrating His kingdom among them. As we do, they will come to us seeking to know the truth. We should be mindful and careful to lead them to the knowledge of the Father, so that they too can embark on this journey into His presence.

Notice that the tent had only one entrance point. Everyone enters the camp through the same door. One should not and could not leap over the outer fence of the tent to enter, but had to make their way to the side which had the door in order to enter. Likewise for us today, Jesus is the door by which we all enter the eternal sanctuary. This reference from St. John's gospel makes it plain. Jesus said, "…I am the door of the sheep… by me if any man enter in, he shall be saved…" (Extracted from John 10: 7-8)

The tent was pitched so that the door was always facing the east. The surrounding nations were worshippers of other gods and their temple worship consisted of them facing the east to worship the sun. Unlike them, when the Israelite worshippers entered the Tabernacle, they were westward facing, instead of eastward facing, so as not to bear any similarity to pagan worship. In today's church we have no geographical compass point that we are directed to face while worshipping our God. The psalmist in Psalm 121, said "I will lift up mine eyes unto the hills, from whence comes my help…" The children of Israel in their wilderness wanderings were accustomed to lifting up their eyes to behold the glory of God upon the top of Mount Sinai.

As is typical throughout the Old Testament, the Tabernacle in the wilderness is a type of the true Tabernacle not made with hands.

Hebrews 8

¹Now of the things which we have spoken this is the sum: We have such an high priest, who is set on the right hand of the throne of the Majesty in the heavens;

²A minister of the sanctuary, and of the true Tabernacle, which the Lord pitched, and not man.

The gospel church collectively, and each of us individually is the true Tabernacle, which the Lord hath pitched, and not man. The body of Christ, in and by which He made atonement, is the greater and more perfect Tabernacle.

Each of us as individuals are lively stones building up this true sanctuary. Seeing God does not dwell in temples made by hand, our bodies must be consecrated and set apart as temples of worship. We need to consecrate this temple, so that the Holy Spirit will find a place in which to reside. That honors God, and is an act of worship in itself. If we seek to use our bodies in ways that do not honor God, nor entertain His presence, that becomes an abuse of a consecrated vessel.

1 Corinthians 6

> *¹⁹What? know ye not that your body is the temple of the Holy Ghost which is in you, which ye have of God, and ye are not your own?*

> *²⁰For ye are bought with a price: therefore glorify God in your body, and in your spirit, which are God's.*

What does it mean for us to consecrate a vessel? The World Online Dictionary meaning of the word *'consecrate'* is:

- devoted or dedicated to a deity or to some religious purpose;
- exclusively devoted to a deity or to some religious ceremony or use;
- reverently dedicated to some person, purpose, or object.

That is indeed what our bodies are – vessels that are exclusively dedicated to the Master's use. Nothing short of that will bring God glory and excite Him to bless us with His presence. We must give our bodies completely over to His dedicatory service.

Consecrate your body now as we continue on our way.

Chapter 8
Secure Your Travel Document

When one arrives at an airport to board a flight for a trip, they must first check in at the entrance. Now we are afforded the privilege of online check-in for faster processing at the airport. Whether online check-in, kiosk check-in or face to face agent check-in, each traveller needs to have proper documentation in order to proceed to the security check point. While we are at the security check point, we are at the furthest point from our destination. If we satisfactorily get through the security check point, we may proceed to boarding. As we proceed to boarding we are getting closer and closer to our destination. When the aircraft is enroute, we are proceeding even closer until finally we reach our destination.

Recall that as the floorplan of the Tabernacle shows, there was one gate into the outer courts of the Tabernacle. Just inside the gate was a bronze-covered altar of sacrifice. The location of this piece of furnishing was the farthest point from getting into the inner sanctuary known as the 'Holy of Holies'. When matters were satisfactorily dealt with at this altar, then the worshipper could proceed. There was no getting around or avoiding the Bronze Altar when approaching and entering the Tabernacle. In Old Testament times, there was no such thing as entering the Tabernacle of God's presence apart from an encounter with the Brazen Altar. In the same way, we cannot bypass the sacrifice of Christ in our approach to God. There is no such thing as bypassing the cross of Christ and seeking to gain enterance into the presence of God. That would be an exercise in futility.

On this Bronze Altar innocent animals were sacrificed. As a part of the ceremonial proceedings, the worshipper would identify with his sacrifice by placing his hand on the animal. This act was symbolic of the worshipper transferring the guilt of his sins onto the sacrificial animal. The animal was then slain and its blood and carcass were dealt with in the prescribed manner. This demonstrated that the worshipper had paid the price for sins committed and was therefore free to proceed further.

The letter to the Hebrews explains that the blood of bulls and goats could never take away sin:

Hebrews 10

¹For the law having a shadow of good things to come, and not the very image of the things, can never with those sacrifices which they offered year by year continually make the comers thereunto perfect.

²For then would they not have ceased to be offered? because that the worshippers once purged should have had no more conscience of sins. ³But in those sacrifices there is a remembrance again made of sins every year.

⁴For it is not possible that the blood of bulls and of goats should take away sins.

⁵Wherefore when he cometh into the world, he saith, Sacrifice and offering thou wouldest not, but a body hast thou prepared me:

⁶In burnt offerings and sacrifices for sin thou hast had no pleasure.

⁷Then said I, Lo, I come (in the volume of the book it is written of me,) to do thy will, O God.

⁸Above when he said, Sacrifice and offering and burnt offerings and offering for sin thou wouldest not, neither hadst pleasure therein; which are offered by the law;

⁹Then said he, Lo, I come to do thy will, O God. He taketh away the first, that he may establish the second.

¹⁰By the which will we are sanctified through the offering of the body of Jesus Christ once for all.

¹¹And every priest standeth daily ministering and offering oftentimes the same sacrifices, which can never take away sins:

¹²But this man, after he had offered one sacrifice for sins forever, sat down on the right hand of God;

[13]From henceforth expecting till his enemies be made his footstool.

[14]For by one offering he hath perfected forever them that are sanctified.

The above passage illustrates that animal sacrifices were merely 'shadows' of the true sacrifice that could take away sin - Jesus. Just as the animals were slain outside of the Holy Place, Jesus our sacrificial Lamb was slain outside the city wall to give us access to the Holy of Holies. He is the travel document we need to proceed further as we approach God. Everyone who seeks to go on this journey into the presence of the Most High, must accept and secure this offering. This is your only access. Secure your travel document.

The second condition for God to live among His people was illustrated by a large bronze basin of water.

Exodus 30

[17]And the LORD spake unto Moses, saying,

[18]Thou shalt also make a laver of brass, and his foot also of brass, to wash withal: and thou shalt put it between the Tabernacle of the congregation and the altar, and thou shalt put water therein.

[19]For Aaron and his sons shall wash their hands and their feet thereat:

[20]When they go into the Tabernacle of the con-

gregation, they shall wash with water, that they die not; or when they come near to the altar to minister, to burn offering made by fire unto the LORD:

[21]So they shall wash their hands and their feet, that they die not: and it shall be a statute for ever to them, even to him and to his seed throughout their generations.

Here the priests, as representatives of the people, would wash their hands and feet before offering a sacrifice or entering the Holy Place. If they did not wash, they were considered ceremonially unclean and unfit for the service and worship of God.

The gate and the Bronze Altar speak of Christ as the way of salvation. Beyond the Bronze Altar speaks of sanctification. Sanctification is the process by which a believer is made holy, or more like Christ, in this life. As God sanctifies us we begin to see things through His eyes, and think more in line with His mind. As seen in the floorplan of the Tabernacle, this basin is placed between the altar of sacrifice and the tent of the Holy Place. Although our sins are forever forgiven as a result of the sacrificial work of Christ, we need daily cleansing from the defiling effects of sin. Jesus' death has given us the great priviledge of entering into the Tabernacle to offer prayers and praises unto God without the need of an appointed priest as it was in the Old Testament. Not only do we have the authority and the privilege, but we also have the responsibility to wash and remain clean. An act we should do daily, or several times daily when once we are made aware of the defilement of sin.

Hebrews 10

²²Let us draw near with a true heart in full assurance of faith, having our hearts sprinkled from an evil conscience, and our bodies washed with pure water.

YOU SHALL BE HOLY (Ex 28:36)

One meaning of the word 'holy' is to be morally and ethically sound. Holiness is a unique quality of God's character and his followers should be holy as He is holy. The Scribes (professional students of the Law) and Pharisees (antoganists of Jesus) adhered to the letter of the law and observed various ordinances, but Jesus insisted that as worshippers of God, seeking to draw closer into His presence, we have more than an outward show of holiness. Jesus wants us to be morally pure. He wants us to adhere to His standards of conduct, distinguishing between right and wrong, and good and bad.

Another meaning of the word 'holy' is to set apart, or consecrate. It is honoring to God to live a life dedicated to Him, being set apart for His service. A true worshipper will set himself apart unto God and will not knowingly touch anything that will defile him.

There is no place for superficiality or uncleanness in approaching God. Those must be dealt with in true repentance. It is an act of worship to confess (agree with God) sins and get rid of them on a daily basis. No more must sin be in our temple, it must be cleansed at the door. We would think twice before walking into a friend's house with tar or mud on our shoes. Yet we are inclined to try to come into God's presence with hands, hearts, and feet covered with the filth of our disobedience, lust or lukewarmness. Our New Testament washing is done by us applying the Word of God to our hearts, minds and lives. As we cleanse our natural bodies daily, even more so should we seek to cleanse our spiritual bodies.

1 John 1

> *⁵This then is the message which we have heard of him, and declare unto you, that God is light, and in him is no darkness at all.*
>
> *⁶If we say that we have fellowship with him, and walk in darkness, we lie, and do not the truth:*
>
> *⁷But if we walk in the light, as he is in the light, we have fellowship one with another, and the blood of Jesus Christ his Son cleanseth us from all sin.*
>
> *⁸If we say that we have no sin, we deceive ourselves, and the truth is not in us.*
>
> *⁹If we confess our sins, he is faithful and just to forgive us our sins, and to cleanse us from all unrighteousness.*
>
> *¹⁰If we say that we have not sinned, we make him a liar, and his word is not in us.*

It is dishonoring to God to walk around daily with unconfessed sins in our life. Sin is like a dead fly in your anointing oil. It causes it to stink and send up a stench in the nostrils of God. Get rid of it speedily. When we worship the Lord in the beauty of holiness, there is an aroma that ascends up to Him. Anything less than the sweet scent of holy worship is abominable unto the Lord.

In securing your travel document, you should see to it that you keep it safe from defilement. Keep travelling. You are getting closer and closer to your destination.

Chapter 9
You're Getting Close

The Tabernacle was divided in two compartments, the Holy Place and the Holy of Holies. Outside this covered structure was the Courtyard that contained the Bronze Altar and the Bronze Laver (basin). The activities of sacrifices and purifications were all done in the Courtyard and were a necessary part of entering the first compartment of the Tabernacle, The Holy Place. This first compartment contained three items of furnishings:

    i. The Table of Showbread
    ii. The Golden Lampstand
    iii. The Altar of Incense

Whereas, the Courtyard represented the place of Santification, the Holy Place represented the place of Edification and Enlightenment.

When the priests entered the Holy Place, they could see the Altar of Incense at the far end of the room. It was placed right next to the heavy curtain, or veil which separated the Holy Place from the Holy of Holies, the innermost compartment of the Tabernacle. In order to get to the Altar of Incense, the priests had to pass between the Table of Showbread and the Golden Lampstand which were placed opposite each other. There were no windows or other source of light in the Tabernacle, but the lampstand with the candlestick. The Table of Showbread provided food for the priests.

These two pieces of furnishings pictured Christ as our only source of light and nourishment. Christ was revealed to us as 'the word', and he left us His spoken word. Therefore for us as believers, seeking to enter into the secret place of the Most High, the word in us is our source of nourishment and enlightenment.

The revelations that I received of the Holy Place for our twenty first century application are these:

- The Tabernacle must be enclosed
- You shall testify of the goodness of the Lord and show forth His praises continually
- You must become a suppporter of the truth of God
- Bring pure oil for the light and cause the lamp to burn always
- You shall eat those things wherewith the atonement was made
- You must give prayer an elevated place in your life

THE TABERNACLE MUST BE ENCLOSED

The Tabernacle, also known as 'the tent of worship' consisted of two compartments which was well adorned and protected. Outwardly, it looked uninviting, but the interior was rich with color. To an outsider, the godly life doesn't look appealing. But to the person who shows faith in God and follows the pattern for entering into His presence, there is a wonderful discovery on entering in. These articles that serve to feed us and enlighten us and to bring us closer to the Father must be protected.

In most places today, we would not think of leaving our valuables unprotected. We guard our treasures and our homes. Why then would we not guard the treasures that God has provided for us in the Holy Place? To leave our homes opened and unguarded is evidence that there is nothing of value in it. Nothing worth guarding. We always seek to protect that which we value. The word of God that brings light into our darkness and guides us, is of great value to the believer, it is more to us than any earthly treasure.

Now that we have these treasures in our earthen vessels, it is an act of worship for us to protect them. As the body of Christ, we have a responsibility to guard that which was given to us, let there be no unnecessary or indecent exposure.

YOU SHALL TESTIFY OF THE GOODNESS OF THE LORD AND SHOW FORTH HIS PRAISES CONTINUALLY

Moses was commanded to place showbread on the table before the Lord, always. This showbread was twelve loaves of unleavened bread arranged in two rows of six each. It was to be kept before God's presence in the Tabernacle continually. Like the manna in the wilderness, served fresh every morning, the old bread was removed weekly and replaced with fresh bread.

John 6

[26]Jesus answered them and said, Verily, verily, I say unto you, Ye seek me, not because ye saw the

miracles, but because ye did eat of the loaves, and were filled.

[27]Labour not for the meat which perisheth, but for that meat which endureth unto everlasting life, which the Son of man shall give unto you: for him hath God the Father sealed...

[30]They said therefore unto him, What sign shewest thou then, that we may see, and believe thee? what dost thou work?

[31]Our fathers did eat manna in the desert; as it is written, He gave them bread from heaven to eat.

[32]Then Jesus said unto them, Verily, verily, I say unto you, Moses gave you not that bread from heaven; but my Father giveth you the true bread from heaven.

[33]For the bread of God is he which cometh down from heaven, and giveth life unto the world.

[34]Then said they unto him, Lord, evermore give us this bread

[35]And Jesus said unto them, I am the bread of life: he that cometh to me shall never hunger; and he that believeth on me shall never thirst.

In the East, bread had more significance than in the West. Viewed as the staff of life, bread symbolized the nourishment, provision and increase upon which life depended. The twelve loaves were a reminder to the twelve tribes of Israel that as they separated themselves to God, and as they relied on Him for their needs, they could count on being able to eat at the table He prepared for them.

Likewise us. We too can count on God supplying us with 'our daily bread'. This supply includes everything we need to live one day at a time as we continue on this journey into the secret place of the Most High. As the old bread was removed weekly and replaced with fresh bread, so our testimonies of God's goodness must be current, because He is constantly providing for us. It is an act of worship to our God for us to tell of His goodness and his provisions for us. Keep your testimony before the eyes of those within your circle of influence that they may see that the Almighty cares for His own and provides for them.

YOU MUST BECOME A SUPPORTER OF
THE TRUTH OF GOD

A lampstand supports a lamp. The word of God is as a lamp unto our feet that gives us daily directions. You must uphold the word of God so that it will give direction to the lost. Your conduct should reveal the light of God in you, and everything you do or say should reveal its truth. As the lampstand supports the lamp, so shall your conduct support the light of God in you.

Uphold the truth, by your lifestyle.

BRING PURE OIL FOR THE LIGHT AND CAUSE THE LAMP TO BURN CONTINUALLY

Dead flies cause the oil to stink. As a worshipper you need to be clean and transparent. No hidden motives. If you are a supporter of the truth of God, then your actions and your words must be congruent. Since you seek to worship God in spirit and in truth, you should constantly check the purity of your oil. The purity of your motives will cause you to adhere to the word, only then can you make your way prosperous.

See to it also that your lamp burns continually. Once you are on the journey into the secret place of the Most High, slack not your riding. Each day should be moving you closer and closer. Keep the fire burning. You cannot afford to be numbered among the five foolish virgins, who while they were waiting for the bridegroom had their lights to go out, because they had no spare oil with them.

YOU SHALL EAT THOSE THINGS WHEREWITH THE ATONEMENT WAS MADE

Exodus 29

[32]And Aaron and his sons shall eat the flesh of the ram, and the bread that is in the basket by the door of the Tabernacle of the congregation.

[33]And they shall eat those things wherewith the atonement was made, to consecrate and to sanctify them: but a stranger shall not eat thereof, because they are holy.

Here Aaron and his sons were consecrated for service in the Tabernacle, and were given commandment to eat those things wherewith the atonement was made. We too are a body of priests, and each one individually, in that we now offer service unto the Lord.

It is an act of worship unto the Lord to observe the body and blood of Jesus Christ by taking the communion. He was the lamb that was slain for us so that we can now be at one with God. When we come together and commune, we do show His death until He comes and as we do we 're-member' Him. We put Him back together again for the world to see. As a true worshipper, do not refuse the communion of the Lord. Worship without communion is like meat devoid of fat. Sometimes dry.

YOU MUST GIVE PRAYER AN ELEVATED PLACE IN YOUR LIFE

The 'Altar of Incense' was positioned next to the veil that separated the Holy Place from the Most Holy Place or Holy of Holies. It was to be lit from the bronze altar of sacrifice which was located in the Courtyard. To gain entrance into the Holy Place, each entrant had to first offer a sacrifice for sin. That sacrifice preceded that which was offered on the Altar of Incense. One had to first receive cleansing from sin before he was accepted or able to offer worship before God. Jesus' death on the cross has already cleansed us from sin, and has granted us the privilege of approaching God in worship.

The fact that it is on the basis of Jesus' sacrifice that you are able to come into His presence with your prayers, you can come boldly to the throne of grace where you will obtain mercy and find grace to help in time of need. Your entrance into the inner sanctuary is intrinsically linked to your prayers and praises at the Altar of Incense. The Altar of Incense was lit from fire taken from the Bronze Altar of sacrifice. No one is able to offer praises and thanksgiving unto God, unless first having accepted the gift of forgiveness of sins offered at the Bronze Altar of sacrifice. It is with a heart of gratitude that we come to the Altar of Incense to offer the fruit of our lips as a sacrifice unto God.

Your prayers are a sweet smell unto the Lord. They must be fervent because only when they are burned will they release aroma. You are very close now to the Holy of Holies. You need to offer up your sacrifices of praise unto the Holy One fervently. Since the veil of the temple has been removed, you are sitting right in front of His face, give Him your all.

This revelation was so extensive that I have dedicated the next chapter entirely to it.

Chapter 10

Get Ready to Experience a Third-Degree Burn

A PRINCIPLE is a general and fundamental truth that may be used in deciding conduct or choice. God instructed Moses in Exodus 30:1 to make an altar to burn incense on. This should be a part of the furnishings in the Tabernacle in which His presence would dwell. This Altar of Incense, two cubits (approx. 3ft) high, stood higher than any other article of furnishing in the Holy Place. On this altar the priest would burn incense twice daily, morning and evening. The incense that was used for this service was totally forbidden to be used individually for any other purpose anywhere else. It had to be used only in the worship of God in the Holy Place. It was burned on pieces of hot coal which produced a delightful aroma in the Holy Place and had to be kept burning at all times.

The book of Revelation records the events of the end time. This is a book of the New Covenant that includes some principles from the Old Covenant. In Rev. 8, verses 3 & 4 the writer John records seeing an angel appearing and standing before an altar having a golden censer. Much incense was given to him to offer with the prayers of all saints upon the golden altar which was before the throne. The smoke of the incense, which came with the prayers of the saints, ascended up before God out of the angel's hand.

We can learn from the foregoing that the prayers of the saints transcend both Old and New Testaments. Here is one act, one principle from Old Testament worship that we can adopt in our New Testament worship. Not that we are commanded to build an altar to offer incense on, but our prayers should forever be ascending to God in worship. In like manner that the Altar of Incense was the most elevated of all the furnishings in the Tabernacle, even so we should give prayer an elevated place in our life. We do so, in the sense that we give it a place of importance, a place of prominence. Communion with our Heavenly Father must be given a well-respected place in our life. Prayer is bi-lateral communication with God and He reveals His mind and His will to us when we pray. If we do not give prayer the place of prominence in our lives that it deserves, we tend to lead fragmented lives, without constant communication with our creator.

In the Old Testament, the incense produced a fragrant aroma constantly before God. Our prayers should come from a heart that burns with love for Him. In appreciation and thanksgiving for all that He is and has done for us and continues to do. It should be heartfelt and passionate. The last clause of James 5:16 states, "The effectual fervent prayer of a righteous man availeth much." Since fervent means to have or show great warmth or intensity, this implies that something has to be burning.

PRAYERS AS INCENSE

Our prayers of praise and thanksgiving must be lifted up to our Heavenly Father. As it was with the Jewish priest who would stand in front of the golden prayer altar and burn fragrant incense twice a day, so must we as believers position ourselves before our Heavenly Father daily. We should come before him offering up praise and thanksgiving letting our petitions be known.

As was mentioned earlier, in the book of Revelation, chapters 5 and 8, we learn that our prayers are as incense before the Lord. They come up before him as a sweet smell. For those of us living in the Western world, incense does not hold the same significance as it does to our counterparts living in the East. In the East, incense was often burned as an expression of honor and recognition for kings and dignitaries. As born again believers in Jesus Christ, the Trinity holds a very high place of honor and recognition for us. They mean more to us than any earthly king or dignitary. As in the Tabernacle, the priest faced the Holy of Holies, when offering sacrifice on the Altar of Incense, even so should we, as children of God turn our hearts towards God continually as we honor Him with our prayers of praise and thanksgivings.

Incense must be burned in order for it to release its odor. In order for our prayer to release an odor that God can smell, it has to be burning, figuratively speaking. It has to be a fervent prayer. And we know that a fervent prayer is effective (James 5:16b). An effectual fervent prayer does not necessarily mean a noisy prayer, but one that burns with passion. A prayer that is ardent; possessing great warmth of feeling. A prayer that is released in faith, grounded in the word of God is a prayer that exhibits enthusiasm, zeal, conviction, persistence and belief.

To *burn* means to be consumed with strong emotions. Our emotion is our mental and psychological state which is associated with our thoughts and behavior, and is a rather subjective experience. Based upon our belief of the scriptures, when we pray, we should be consumed with confidence, excitement, pleasure and expectation. We know that He hears us always and grants us the desires of our hearts based upon His will, which is revealed in the written word. Our prayers need to ascend to God, and unless they are consumed by fire, they have not yet left our altars. We must feel the intensity and seriousness of our prayers. They need to be set on fire.

BURN CLASSIFICATIONS

Burns are classified in order of increasing seriousness. The most common system of classifying burns categorizes them as first, second or third-degree depending on how deep or severe they penetrate the skin's surface. Sometimes this is extended to include a fourth or even up to a sixth degree, but most burns are first to third degree.

- First-degree burns damage only the outer layer of skin and produces redness.

- Second-degree burns damage the outer layer and the layer underneath and produce blisters.

- Third-degree burns damage or destroy the deepest layer of skin and tissues underneath. This also destroys and chars the skin tissues.

Burns totally destroy the body's ability to regulate its processes. The worst pain from a burn comes with second degree burns because the nerve endings are left exposed, and resulting in throbbing, intense pain. Third degree burns are worse than second degree burns, but actually hurt less, since protective sensation has been interrupted by the burn.

It is necessary to draw some similarities here between the

various degrees of burns and our prayers. In a first degree burn, either due to proximity, the length of exposure, or the strength of the fire, the victim suffers damage to the outer layer of the skin only. The Bible teaches that man is a tri-partite being, consisting of spirit, soul and body. When a person goes through the motion of praying that involves his flesh only, he is merely warming himself by the fire much like Peter did on the night of Jesus' trial before his crucifixion. He is not fully engulfed by his prayer. His prayer is probably not mixed with faith and he is simply going through a physical exercise to ease the conscience. He is experiencing just a slight redness of skin, and in some cases literally so depending on his posture during prayer.

A person with a second degree burn is in a great deal of pain due to exposed nerve endings. The outer layer has been burnt off and there is no protective layer over the nerves. When we pray to the extent where we begin to see ourselves through the light of the scriptures, without any commitment to adjust our behavior, we have entered into a painful place. Painful because we are at enmity within ourselves, and cognitive dissonance will reap havoc with the soul. It is impossible to serve God along with anything else. In doing so, one is constantly torn apart. One part of us wants to draw close to God, and the other pulling away from him. When we see ourselves in prayer and commit our ways to the Father so he can work the work of righteousness in us, the toiling is over. Now we are completely dead to the flesh. The outer layer is burned off and our life is hid with God in Christ. That's a place of peace.

As was noted earlier, a second degree burn hurts worse than a third degree burn. In a third degree burn the nerve endings are consumed and therefore does not feel pain as much as a second degree burn. With respect to prayer and our communication with God, we all need to experience a third degree burn. When we pray, we need to be so passionate about our prayer and have so much confidence and faith in the one to whom we pray, that we totally relinquish all to Him. Our prayer has to get to that place where it causes something to happen. We do need to pray like we had a third degree burn.

Our prayer must come from a heart that is being poured out to God, one that is constantly being purged from iniquity. Ps 66:18 teaches that those who regard iniquity in their heart will not be heard when they pray. Those who deviate from right, and deny the sovereignty of God, holding to no spiritual value and following a path of lawlessness, have no guarantee of answered prayers. The Lord will not hear the prayer of those who practice sin. 'Practice' is the operative word in that statement. Constantly doing and making it a lifestyle. We must remain in the presence of the 'Son'. In so doing the light that exudes from him will burn away iniquity. We need a third-degree 'son' burn. One that burns away our flesh and leaves us opened to God.

SON-BURN

Every so often we smell the sweet aroma of burning flesh, especially at a holiday barbeque. Whenever that smell hits our nostril we begin to salivate. If we are a part of the festivities, we look forward to having a sumptuous meal and sometimes get very anxious about it. If we are not, then we wish we were.

Burned flesh is a sweet smell before God. He too delights in the aroma of burned flesh. Our prayers need to consume our flesh. We approach God in humility, but we should be passionate about doing so. We go boldly before His throne. As our flesh is consumed, our spirit comes alive.

One way that one sustains a burn is by being exposed to a source of heat. So is the case of sunburn. Too much exposure to the sun's rays will cause the skin to burn. Exposure to the love rays of the 'SON' (Jesus) will cause a 'SON-burn'. Once you've been exposed to Jesus, others will know that you have been with Him. Peter denied being with him but his speech betrayed him. Moses came down from the mountain after spending in excess of forty days in the presence of God, and his face glowed. The frequency and the duration of your contact with Him will also determine the classification of your burn. In the dictionary we see certain synonyms that are associated with the word 'burn'. Words such as scorch, singe, sear, char, parch. We will look at each of these separately.

SCORCH

One gets scorched whenever they come in contact with flame or heated metal. Usually it is a superficial burn. It is a slight surface burn. Slight, in the sense that it is weak; not decidedly marked; not forcible. It is inconsiderable, unimportant and insignificant. It is not considered a severe burn. One would experience skin discoloration, possible damaged texture and some brittleness.

If a structure is on fire anything that is in close proximity to it will be scorched. There are dynamics that will determine whether or not a building in close proximity to a burning building will indeed catch on fire itself. Being in the presence of fervent prayer bears the same similarity. You may get your emotions aroused but no real involvement. You have a surface relationship with the son. You need to experience a burn beyond getting chill bumps and falling out. If you are in the presence of corporate prayer but you have no real involvement you are only being scorched.

SINGE

This is a superficial and momentary burning of edges through nearness to the heat source. For the moment you may be tantalized, but as soon as you are removed from the source, the emotion changes. In the agricultural industry, poultry and pork is singed to remove stub feathers and bristles. In the textile industry, loose fibers protruding on the surface of textile goods are singed to remove them.

There are those among us that are always soliciting the prayers of others but never practice praying on their own. Whenever they are experiencing a crisis they solicit prayers. I am in no way speaking against them doing so, but if that is the only time you pray, then you are only been singed. The prayer is removing a seemingly negative situation, but no real change is experienced.

SEAR

In culinary art searing is a cooking technique which quickly cooks the exterior of a food item. The interior remains unchanged. Sear is described as a scar produced by burning of organic tissue as in the case of branding and cauterization.

In English Lexicon, the word brand originally meant anything hot or burning, such as a firebrand, a burning stick. By the European Middle Ages it commonly identified the process of burning a mark into stock animals with thick hides, such as cattle, so as to identify ownership. Cauterization is a medical term describing the burning of the body to remove or close a part of it. With both of these terms, as it is also with the cooking technique, only a part of the object is affected.

If you are branded it shows that you belong, but it does not necessarily mean that you are surrendered. As in the case of the Tabernacle, one could not remain in the Courtyard and experience the objects that lie further in. In order for us to enter the holy of holies we must proceed into the Tabernacle. A Christian that does not exercise his right to enter in has not fully given of himself to the Lord in communion and service. Praying like this is praying but not believing that we have what we ask. We might repeat a prayer just to satisfy the conscience or some ritual but we are not fully involved.

CHAR

Char means to burn something to charcoal. It is the solid material that remains after light gases and tar have been driven-out or released from a carbonaceous material, during the initial stage of combustion. It is the reduction of a burning substance to carbon. In many ancient languages it is a term for death.

When a material is charred, it has undergone a total change –a metamorphosis. The new substance no longer resembles the old. Prayer must bring about change in us and can certainly cause changes in our circumstances and situations. We have heard it over and over again that "Prayer changes things". That is a true and faithful saying, but only prayer that has its foundation in the word of God and that is mixed with faith. It is not the volume of the prayer. In the book of First Samuel, Hannah prayed silently before the Lord and he heard her and granted her petition. It is the fervency, intensity and passion of it. It is a firm belief in the ability of God to grant our petition because it is in accordance with his revealed will as found in the scriptures. Such prayers will produce change. Because it is done passionately, the 'pray-er' has given himself over to the prayer.

Coal is a rock that has been changed from its original state due to exposure to elevated temperature and pressure. When I was a child, I witnessed my parents setting up a 'coal-kiln' to burn coal from wood. The wood was covered with dirt and lit. It was left to burn for days in order to produce the coal. My parents would always check to see that the fire kept burning. In like manner, we should seclude ourselves from time to time. We should remain in His presence for extended periods, exposing ourselves to Him. Being in His presence will change us. The longer we stay is the more we will be changed. Prayer will reduce our flesh to nothingness. It will change its desires. As it were, our flesh will experience a metamorphosis. Like the resulting coal, the dross will be burned out of our lives. Whenever that takes place we will have a sustained desire to see the lives of others changed and will intercede for them passionately.

PARCH

The verb form of the word 'parch' means to make someone very thirsty, or to make very dry. When the ground is exposed to the effects of the sun for an extended period of time without water, it tends to crack. Considering that we are 'earth', we too after prolonged exposure to the 'son' will experience breaking. In the garden of Gethsemane, Jesus was so intense in prayer that His sweat became as if it were drops of blood. In His human form, He too experienced breaking. Even though He was God, yet in human flesh His will still had to be broken. He prayed "Father if it is possible, let this cup pass from me, nevertheless, not my will but thine be done."

We must be consistent in prayer, and so passionate about that which we pray so that like Jesus we too experience breaking. Our will and of all our fleshly desires need to be broken. Our prolonged exposure to the son will produce openings in us to receive the oil of the Lord. As we remain in His presence, He will fill us as we become open to receiving from Him.

In the Beatitudes, Jesus teaches us that if we hunger and thirst after righteousness, we will be filled. David's prayer in Ps 141 includes this petition, "Let my prayer be set forth before thee as incense; and the lifting up of my hands as the evening sacrifice." Our prayers are as incense before the Lord and should never go out before Him.

You are right at the place now for Him to stretch forth His hand and bring you into that which you longed for – a revelation of His divine presence. That which you have sought for;   to experience the fullness of His presence and to be brought into the secret place of the Most High.

Chapter 11

Go on In, It's Open

Through your continuous prayers, praise, worship and adoration of your God, from a heart that has been cleansed from sin, you have now been brought nigh unto His presence. In the floorplan of the Tabernacle, you are now approaching the most holy place, The Holy of Holies. Along the way you have had great experiences and enjoyed the journey. You now arrive at this place to realize that there is no longer a partition preventing you from entering the secret place of the Most High.

As you stand in amazement at His awsome presence, you are reminded of the symbolic furnishings of this place and rejoice to know that you are standing now where once only the high priest stood once yearly. This is the place you have longed for.

Behind the now-absent veil once stood the gold-covered 'treasure chest' which was the only piece of furnishing in this compartment. It was made to house the two stone tablets of the law. On top of the chest was a golden cover called the mercy seat. Attached to the ends of the cover were golden images of heavenly creatures called 'cherubims' which stood guard to protect the contents of the chest:

- The tablets of the law that were brought down from Sinai by Moses
- A pot of manna
- Aaron's rod that budded.

Here you stand, being drawn into the presence of the Most Holy God contemplating the symbolism only to realize that just as the treasure chest was the only piece of furnishing in this place, so are you before God. You are standing in His presence removed from the crowd. Seeing that you have already grown accustomed to adoring Him, I doubt you will be standing. You are on your face before Him in humble adoration. You are thankful that you've found an opened door where you can walk right in before the presence of the God whom you adore.

The tablet of the law is now written on the table of your heart. Whereas once they were broken in disgust of sin, now you have hidden them in a protective place, and can now say with the psalmist, "Thy word have I hid in my heart that I might not sin against you". The word that has guided you and directed you all throughout this journey is now been illuminated by the light of His presence. You are now receiving new revelations. You feel as if you have stepped into the dawning of an entirely new day.

As you contemplate the pot of manna, you are once again reminded of His constant provision for you. You rejoice when you remember how He had provided for you miraculously along the way. Never did you go a day without Him supplying your daily bread. You have been well provided for and have eaten sumptuously from His table, even in the presence of your enemies. While you are still contemplating, you recall also how He anointed your head with oil and caused your cup to run over. You have experienced His guidance and protection throughout your journey, and want to express your gratitude. You lift your hand in a wave of His glory and shout unto Him in a voice of triumph. Surely goodness and mercy have followed you and you now intend to dwell in this place forever.

As you recall Him giving back life to Aaron's rod and caused it to bud again, you thank Him for life. Natural life that He has given you but even more so for the brand new life that He affords you through His son. You just want to thank Him for everything, so you lift your voice even higher than before in a resounding prayer of thankfulness:

> *Blessed are you Oh God and Father of my Lord and Savior Jesus Christ, who has blessed me with all spiritual blessings in heavenly places in Christ.*
>
> *Father I thank you for choosing me in Christ before the foundation of the world to be holy and without blame in love. Thank you for making me accepted in the beloved and have given me redemption through His blood and the forgiveness of sin through the riches of His grace.*
>
> *Father I thank you for the inheritance that I have obtained through Christ that I should be to the praise of His glory, being sealed with the Holy Spirit of promise.*
>
> *Father I pray that you will give me the spirit of wisdom and revelation in the knowledge of your son Jesus. Open the eyes of my understanding and enlighten me that I may know what is the hope of His calling and riches of the glory of His inheritance.*
>
> *Father, Oh that I may know what is the exceeding greatness of your power towards us who*

believe according to the working of your mighty power which you wrought in Christ when you raised Him from the dead and set Him at your right hand in heavenly places far above all principalities and power and might and dominion and every name that is named not only in the world but also in that which is to come.

Father you have put all things under His feet, and gave Him to be the head over all things to the church which is His body, the fullness of Him that continues to fill all in all.

Thank you for giving life to me who was dead in trespasses and sins, wherein in times past I walked according to the course of this world. Thank you for delivering me from the lust of my flesh, so that I no longer fulfill the desires of the flesh and of the mind and I am no longer a child of wrath.

Father thank you for your mercy and your great love wherewith you loved me and even though I was dead you raised me up together with Christ and allowed me to sit in heavenly places with Him. Father in the ages to come I look forward to seeing the exceeding riches of your grace in your kindness towards me in Christ Jesus.

Thank you for giving me the gift of salvation. Thank you that I am now drawn close to you and there is now no enmity between us.

Thank you that I am no more a foreigner but a citizen of your great household and kingdom. I will forever praise your name.

Amen.   *(Scripture reference: Ephesians 1 & 2)*

I suspect you are at a point now where you are so engulfed in the beauty of His presence and the fact that He takes delight in you being in His secret place, that you no longer want to hear any other voice but His.

So at this point, I will not disturb you. I'll leave you to enjoy the glory of His presence. You have been a wonderful travelling companion.

Notes

_____

_____

_____

_____

_____

_____

_____

_____

_____

_____

_____

_____

_____

_____

_____

_____

_____

_____

_____

_____

_____

_____

_____

_____

_____

_____

_____

_____

_____

_____

_____

_____

_____

_____

_____

_____

_____

_____

_____

_____

_____

_____

_____

_____

_____

_____

_____

_____

_____

_____

_____

_____

_____

_____

_____

_____

_____

_____

_____

_____

_____

_____

_____

_____

_____

_____

_____

_____

_____

_____

_____

_____

_____

_____

_____

_____

_____

_____

_____

_____

_____

_____

_____

_____

_____

_____

_____

_____

_____

_____

_____

_____

_____

_____

_____

_____

_____

_____

_____

_____

www.ingramcontent.com/pod-product-compliance
Lightning Source LLC
Chambersburg PA
CBHW071013040426
42443CB00007B/757